How to use Early Days

Early Days has been designed to help parents to teach simple Bible truths in an exciting and practical way.

Choose a quiet area to work and have the materials (if any) needed for the activity at hand. You will find it most helpful to use the Good News Bible as this is the version that the *Early Days* notes are based upon.

Read the Bible verse and then the story, and try to involve your child as much as possible. Encourage him/her to talk about the reading and the story and add your own comments. Try to help your child understand the theme.

Take time to do the activity for the day, but don't worry if you can't finish it or if you miss a few days. It's better to "get together" every other day for a longer time than to rush every day.

After you have completed the activity, say the prayer at the bottom of the page. Encourage your child to add to this prayer time, perhaps including people or situations that you think are relevant.

= Bible reading   = Prayer

EARLY DAYS
with Jesus
Big Activity Book

Nan Drew

Mum

Dad

Gran Ross

Grandpa Ross

Matthew

Barry

Ben

Kate

Sparks

Fun to Use Bible Activity Book
to help you grow with God

In the beginning, God made the world.

Colour-in

 Thank You, God, for making the world.

Then God made the sea.

Cut out patches of blue from old magazines to make a sea collage.

 **Thank You, God, for the sea.**

After making the world, God made the plants and trees to make it beautiful.

Find the right homes for these plants.

 **Thank You, God, for making a beautiful world.**

God then made the birds and fishes.

Colour all the fishes blue and all the birds red.

Thank You, God, for the birds and fishes.

After the birds and fishes, God made the animals to live on the land.

Draw lines to make pairs.

 **Thank You, God, for animals.**

God made a man and woman to take care of the world.

Cut out man and woman (see back of book – 1) and stick to picture.

Thank You, God, for making Adam and Eve.

A long time afterwards, God sent people to different parts of the world.

Help these people to get to their new homes.

 **Thank You, God, for all the different people in Your world.**

This is the Ross family.

Colour-in

Thank You, God, for my family.

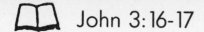 John 3:16-17

God sent Jesus to tell people about Him. This is Jesus' family.

Colour-in

 **Dear Jesus, please take care of my family.**

It's good to know we are all part of God's family.

me

Colour-in

 **Thank You, Jesus, that I am part of Your family.**

The Ross family live in a house. It has three bedrooms, a bathroom, lounge and kitchen-diner. They also have a garden to play in. What sort of house do you live in?

Colour-in

 **Thank You, God, for my house.**

In Jesus' time, most houses only had one room. The animals lived at one end and the family lived at the other. There was a raised platform where they slept. When it was hot at night, they often slept on the roof.

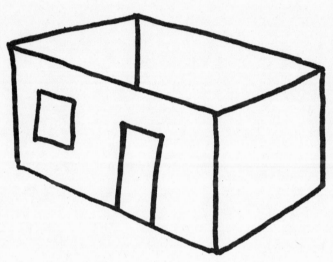

Make a model house

You will need a shoe box or similar. Cut out holes for windows and door. Inside, cut part of the lid to make the raised area where the family lived. Stick the inside of a match box for the manger from which the animals ate their food.

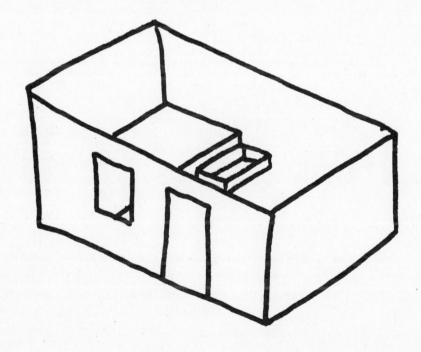

 **Thank You, God, for all the different homes people make.**

The Rosses have nice neighbours next door. Claire often pops in for a cup of tea and sometimes takes Ben and Kate to school and playschool.

In which houses do these neighbours live?

 Thank You, God, for neighbours.

Old Mrs Lloyd is very kind and Mum often gets her pension for her and does odd bits of shopping.

Can you name all the things on the list?

 Dear Jesus, show me how I can be helpful.

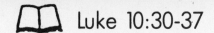 Luke 10:30-37

Jesus tells us that everyone is our neighbour, not just the people next door, or across the road.

Colour-in

 Dear Jesus, help me to be a kind neighbour.

 Mark 11:1-10

Looking out of the window, Ben and Kate can see the whole of the street they live in – not only the people but also the crossing, the traffic lights and the shop on the corner.

Make a street scene (see back of book – 2).

 Thank You, God, for my street and the people who live in it.

Ben and Kate live in a town, which is a place with lots of houses, shops and factories.

Cut out pictures of buildings from magazines.

 **Dear Jesus, please keep me safe when there are lots of cars and people about.**

When the weather is fine, Mum takes Ben and Kate to the park.

Stick on wool for swing ropes.

 **Thank You, God, for nice days in the park.**

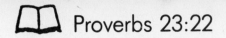 Proverbs 23:22

On the way home, they call at Nan's flat for a drink and a biscuit.

Draw a picture of your favourite snack.

 Please, God, keep old people safe.

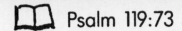

Sometimes at weekends, Dad takes Ben and Kate swimming. Ben can just about swim on his own, but Kate still uses armbands. It's great fun, but Kate doesn't like it when people splash!

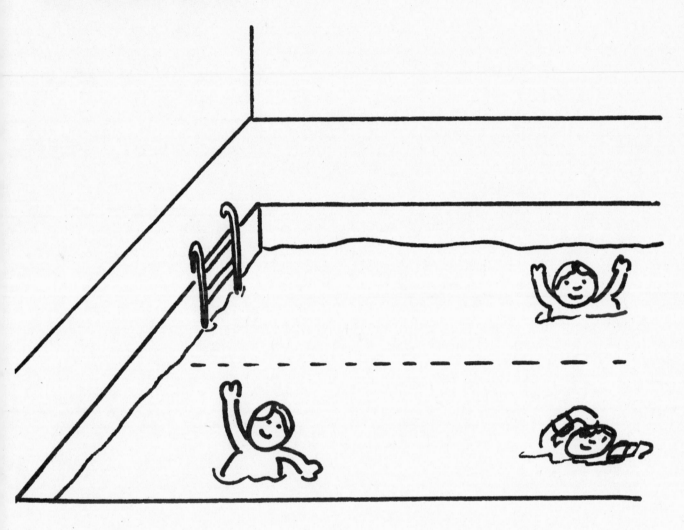

Cut out (see back of book – 3) and cut slot to 'swim'.

 Dear Jesus, help me to be kind and thoughtful.

Nan goes to the same church as all the Ross family. They have lots of friends there. It's good to feel part of God's family.

Draw a picture of your church.

Thank You, God, that I am part of Your family.

Genesis 2:8-10

Gran and Grandpa live in the country with lots of fields and trees all around. Just down the road is the village which is only a few houses, a church, and a small shop.

Stick on scraps for leaves.

 Thank You, God, for the countryside You made.

Gran and Grandpa live on a farm. They keep ducks, chickens, cows and sheep.

Make a cow from a toilet roll and straws.

 **Dear Jesus, please keep farmers safe as they look after the animals.**

In their fields they grow wheat, some cabbages, and lots of grass for the animals.

Finger paint a picture of fields.

 **Thank You, God, that You provide food for everyone.**

Jesus lived in a village called Nazareth, which is in the hills near Lake Galilee.

Colour-in

 Dear God, thank You for Jesus.

A stream runs through Gran and Grandpa's farm. The ducks enjoy swimming in it and Ben and Kate paddle and fish in it when they go to stay.

Help the children to catch the fish.

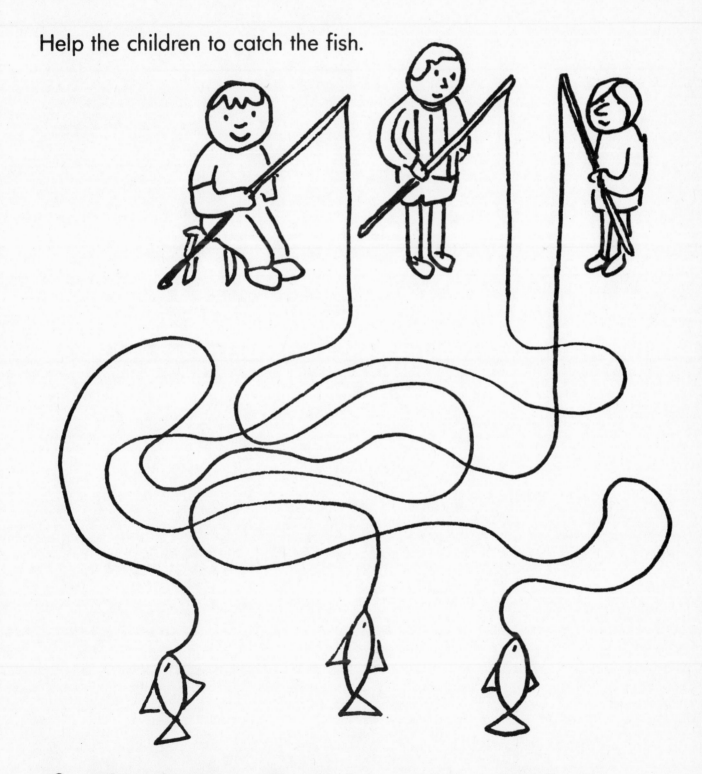

 Thank You, God, for water which we can enjoy.

The stream flows into a big river, which runs into the sea. Ben and Kate went to the seaside for their holidays.

Stick on silver paper for water.

Thank You, God, for holidays.

Ben and Kate live in England, which is an island, so there is sea all around it.

What do you think an island looks like? Draw a picture.

 Thank You, God, for the sea and the fish that live in it.

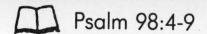 Psalm 98:4-9

England is only a small part of the world. There are many more countries with sandy deserts, high mountains and large lakes.

Colour-in

 **Thank You, God, that You created so many different places.**

Isn't it good that God made such a variety of places for His people to live in?

What places are these?

I _ _ _ _ _ _

M _ _ _ _ _ _ _ _ _ _

S _ _ _ _ _ _ _

C _ _ _ _ _ _ _ _ _ _ _ _

 **Thank You, God, that You made me.**

Best Friends

Fun to Use Bible Activity Book to help you grow with God

Ben's best friend was coming to tea. They were having beefburger and chips followed by ice cream – they were Tom's favourite. When they got home from school they went up to Ben's room to play with his cars, and after tea they went back up to play a game.

Make a collage of your favourite foods with pictures cut out of magazines.

 Thank You, God, for friends.

Ben and Tom walk to school together. Their Mums meet outside the paper shop on the corner. Kate walks along with the pram but Ben and Tom walk together.

Cut out wheels (see back of book – 4) and attach with split pins.

 Dear Jesus, please help me to make special friends.

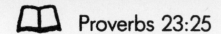 Proverbs 23:25

Tom's Dad took the two boys to a football match. It was great, but very cold; their team won 2-1.

Cut slot to swing leg (see back of book – 5).

 Thank You, God, for football matches.

After the match they had fish and chips and Ben stayed the night. Ben slept in Tom's bed and Tom slept on the floor in a sleeping bag. They talked for a long time and before they went to sleep they had a 'midnight feast'.

Stick on scraps.

 **Dear Jesus, please keep me safe when I sleep away from home.**

Saul's son Jonathan was deeply attracted to David and came to love him as much as he loved himself. Saul kept David with him from that day on and did not let him go back home. Jonathan swore eternal friendship with David because of his deep affection for him. He took off the robe he was wearing and gave it to David, together with his armour and also his sword, bow, and belt.

Colour-in.

 Dear Jesus, please show me how I can share with my friends.

Ben took Tom along to Club at the church. They were both in the same group and were making a model of Noah's Ark.

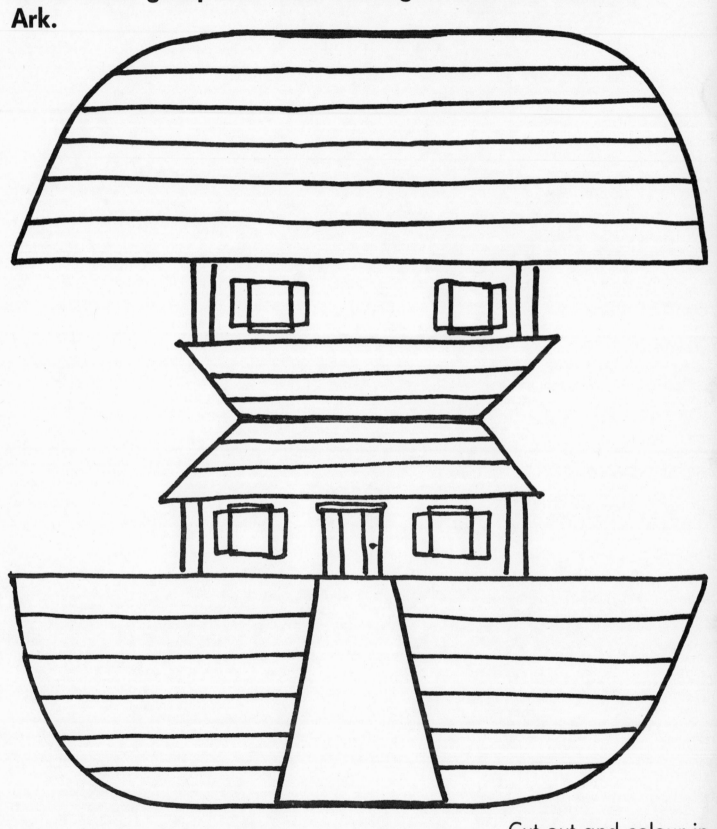

Cut out and colour-in.

 Dear Jesus, please help me to invite my friends to church.

Kate and Dad had gone to meet Ben. He was very late coming out. Then they saw Tom's Mum waiting too and guessed the boys were together. At last they appeared. Ben had lost his coat and Tom had helped him search. He'd found it behind some chairs in the corner!

Find Ben's coat.

 **Thank You, God, for friends who help us.**

David lived in King Saul's palace and played his harp for him, but Saul was very bad-tempered and began to hate David. He told Jonathan to kill him but Jonathan loved David so he decided to help him escape instead.

Colour-in.

 Thank You, God, for friends who care about me.

Jonathan sent David to hide behind a big stone in the fields. He said he would talk to his father and then come and let David know if it was safe to return.

Colour-in.

Thank You, God, for friends who do things for me.

Jonathan was going to shoot three arrows towards the big stone. If he told the servant that they were beside it, then David would know it was all right, but if he said that the arrows were ahead of him, then David must leave.

Colour-in.

 Dear Jesus, please help me to be patient when I have to wait.

Jonathan went to his father and begged him not to kill David but Saul wouldn't listen. He just got more angry and even threw a sword at Jonathan!

Colour-in.

 **Dear Jesus, please protect me when others get angry.**

When Jonathan came back to the field, the signal he gave was for David to go. David was very sad but Jonathan came to say goodbye and they promised always to stay friends.

Colour-in.

 Dear Jesus, please be with me when I am feeling sad.

At breakfast time Mum was busy reading a letter. It was from a lady called Sue who lived in America. She had been at school with Mum. She was in England visiting her mother and wanted to come and see them.

Post the letters in the letter box, cut slot, cut out letters (see back of book – 6).

Thank You, God, for letters.

Sue had been a good friend to Mum at school. They had had lots of fun. After breakfast Mum found some old photos. This was Mum, Sue and Pat (Mum's friend who lived on the other side of town) on a school trip. This was them in the school play and this was Pat, Sue and another girl playing hockey.

Colour-in. Ask mummy if she has any pictures of her school days.

 **Thank You, God, for memories.**

Proverbs 23:11

Mum had lots of memories of school. Mum told Ben and Kate about their school uniform and about the time the door handle came off and they were all trapped! School had been fun! Mum would like to see Sue again.

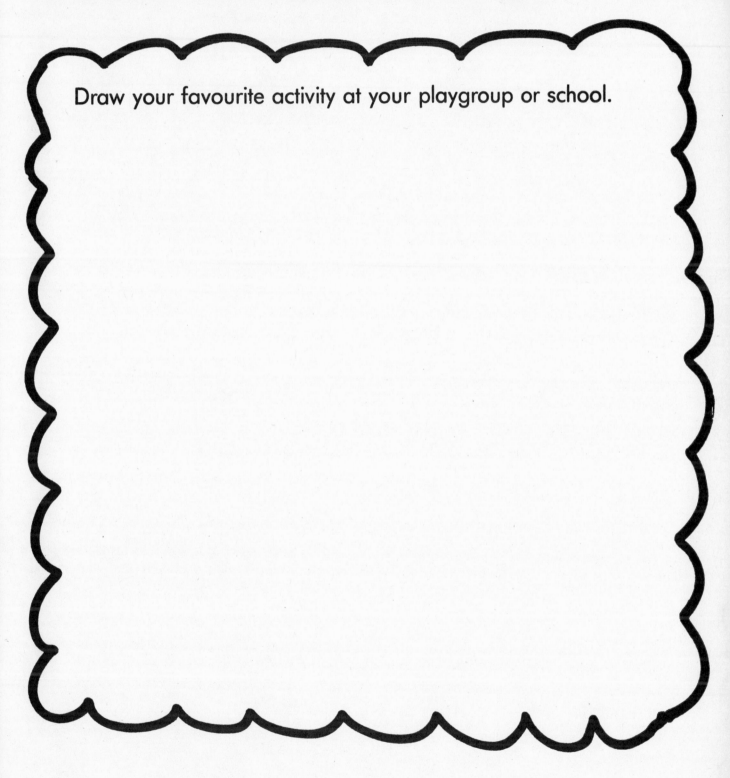

Draw your favourite activity at your playgroup or school.

Thank You, God, for school.

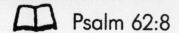

Next day a phone call came. It was Sue. Could Sue and Mum meet? Mum was so excited but now she sounded shy. Mum arranged for Sue to come the next day and Pat would come too.

Cut out and thread cotton to make telephone (see back of book – 7).

 **Dear Jesus, please help me when I feel shy.**

Proverbs 3:27

When Sue arrived, Mum introduced Dad and the children, but soon the photos were out again and the family were forgotten. Dad took Ben and Kate out for a walk with Barry. When they got back the three ladies were laughing and giggling but Sue gave Ben and Kate a hug and showed them pictures of her children and their cat at home in America.

Stick on scraps.

Dear Jesus, please take care of people who are far away from their families.

📖 Proverbs 27:10a

When it was time to leave, Mum was very sad but they promised to go on writing and sending Christmas cards. Sue and Mum had been friends for a long time even though they were far away from each other.

Cut slot. Cut out 'arm' to wave (see back of book – 8).

 Dear Jesus, please help me to remember my friends.

As they grew up, David and Jonathan went on being friends, although they did not see each other very much.

Colour-in.

 **Thank You, God, that some friends go on and on.**

Years later when Saul and Jonathan were killed in battle, David was very sad. He tore his clothes and wrote a song about how much he loved Jonathan.

Colour-in.

 Dear Jesus, please help me when I am feeling sad.

Ben came in from school very grumpy. He went up to his room and slammed the door. He had fallen out with Tom. They weren't friends any more. Tom wouldn't share his marbles.

Cut out the happy face, roll around a pencil. Place over other picture then move up and down (unrolling the picture) and see the face change.

 Dear Jesus, please forgive me when I'm feeling grumpy.

Next day Ben ignored Tom outside the shop and, although the Mums walked together, the boys didn't speak. Nor did they speak all day at school or on the way home. Kate thought it was all very silly!

Help Ben and Tom get to their homes.

 **Dear Jesus, please help me not to be silly.**

Next day Ben began to feel lonely. Tom was playing football with some of the other boys but Ben was on his own in the playground. He nearly asked to join in but he didn't.

Find six differences in these pictures.

 Dear Jesus, please help me when I'm feeling lonely.

Jesus told this parable:

"There was once a man who had two sons. The younger one said to him, 'Father, give me my share of the property now.' So the man divided his property between his two sons. After a few days the younger son sold his part of the property and left home with the money."

Colour-in.

 Dear Jesus, please help me not to be greedy.

"He went to a country far away, where he wasted his money in reckless living. He spent everything he had. Then a severe famine spread over that country, and he was left without a thing. So he went to work for one of the citizens of that country, who sent him out to his farm to take care of the pigs. He wished he could fill himself with the bean pods the pigs ate, but no one gave him anything to eat."

Colour-in

 Dear Jesus, please take care of people who don't have enough food.

"At last he came to his senses and said, 'All my father's hired workers have more than they can eat, and here I am about to starve! I will get up and go to my father and say, Father, I have sinned against God and against you. I am no longer fit to be called your son; treat me as one of your hired workers.' So he got up and started back to his father."

Colour-in.

 Dear Jesus, please help me to be sensible.

"He was still a long way from home when his father saw him; his heart was filled with pity, and he ran, threw his arms round his son, and kissed him."

Colour-in.

 Thank You, God, for my family.

Ben was all smiles when he came out of school. He had made up with Tom. They had shared some sweets at lunchtime, played cars together and now they were asking what time they were going to club!

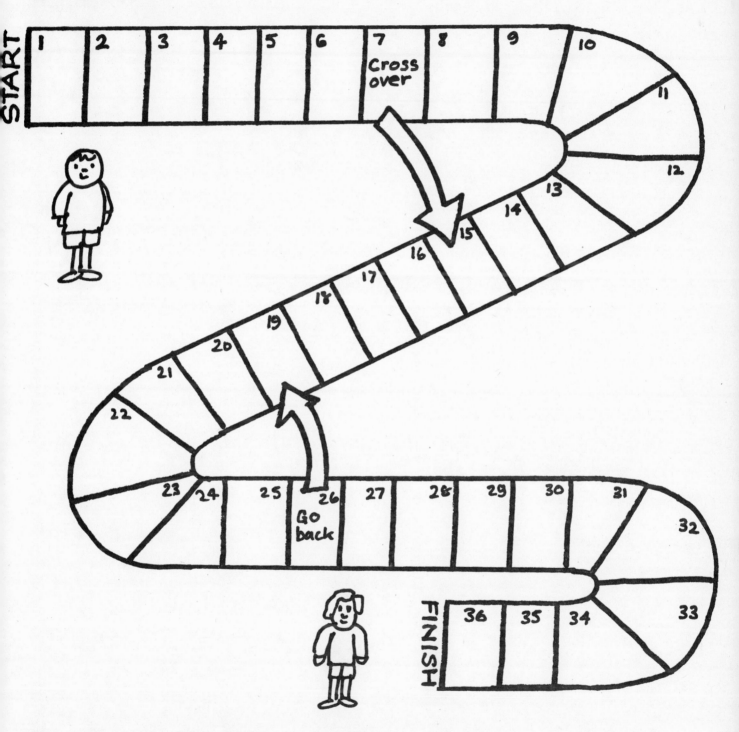

You will need a dice and counter. To play: Throw 1, go forward two spaces. Throw 2, miss a turn. 3, go back one space. 4, go forward one space. 5, go back two spaces. 6, go forward three spaces.

 Dear Jesus, please help me to make up after an argument.

It is good to have a friend. Jesus is the best friend you can have. He is always there, never leaves you and never lets you down.

Colour-in.

 Thank You, Jesus, that You are my friend.

Jesus even died on the cross for us so that God would forgive all our sins and everything that we do wrong.

Colour-in.

 Thank You, Jesus, for dying for me.

People Who Care

**Fun to Use Bible Activity Book
to help you grow with God**

Ben and Kate woke up early. They could hear the dustbin lorry coming. They rushed to the window, then waved to the dustbin men. Collecting everybody's rubbish can't be much fun but the men always seem happy and cheerful.

Two of these dustbins are the same, which ones?

 **Thank You, Jesus, for people who are willing to do messy jobs.**

While Ben was in the bathroom and Kate was getting dressed, they could hear the clink of milk bottles. The milkman has to get up very early to collect the milk from the dairy to start his round.

Ben and Kate know where milk comes from – they have often watched Grandpa milking the cows.

Colour-in dots to make picture.

 **Thank You, Jesus, for milkmen who get up early for us.**

As Kate and Ben came downstairs, the letter-box rattled and the post dropped onto the mat. There was a brown envelope for Dad, a card from the library for Mum and a thick letter for everyone! It's a letter from Gran and Grandpa.

Make a pillar box.

Cut a slot in a toilet roll for the letters. Paint the bottom $\frac{1}{3}$ black, rest red. Cut out a circle of card slightly larger than the toilet roll, paint red and stick on top. Draw on door, stick on a piece of white paper for 'times' panel.

 **Dear Jesus, it's fun to get letters and cards – please help me to write to other people.**

After breakfast the children were going out with Mum. Halfway down the road they heard a cheery voice calling out – it was Mike, the window cleaner. He was just getting a bucket of clean water from Mrs Brown.

Cut out arm and attach with split pin (see back of book – 9).

 Thank You, God, for cheery people; help me to be cheerful.

On their way to the shops Mum, Kate and Ben had to cross a busy main road. On school days the lollipop lady is always there to help them. Today PC Proctor was at the crossing.

Cut out sign (see back of book – 10). Stick on a straw for pole.

 Dear God, thank You for people who look after us.

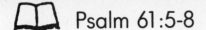

The children both know PC Proctor. He often visits the school and playgroup to talk to the children about road safety and not going off with strangers.

Stick on silver paper for headlights.

 **Dear Jesus, please help me to remember to be careful crossing roads.**

Some men came carrying a paralysed man on a bed, and they tried to take him into the house and put him in front of Jesus. Because of the crowd, however, they could find no way to take him in. So they carried him up on the roof, made an opening in the tiles, and let him down on his bed into the middle of the group in front of Jesus. When Jesus saw how much faith they had, he said to the man, "Your sins are forgiven, my friend."

Colour-in

 Thank You, Jesus, for friends who help us.

The teachers of the Law and the Pharisees began to say to themselves, "God is the only one who can forgive sins!" Jesus knew their thoughts and said to them, "Why do you think such things? I will prove to you, then, that the Son of Man has authority on earth to forgive sins." So he said to the paralysed man, "I tell you, get up, pick up your bed, and go home!" At once the man got up in front of them all, took the bed he had been lying on, and went home, praising God.

Colour-in

Dear Jesus, help me to believe and do what You say.

Around the corner was a car with its bonnet up. As Mum and the children passed, the breakdown truck arrived. They stopped to watch as the mechanic slid himself under the car.

Thread wool through hole and stick on hook (see back of book – 11).

Dear God, take care of people when their cars break down.

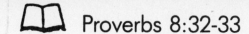

After about five minutes, the man came out from under the car shaking his head, and after a word with the owner he backed up his truck, hooked up the car and towed it off to the garage.

Cut out, stick to hook.

 **Thank You, Jesus, for people who can mend cars.**

📖 Galatians 6:2, 9-10

Mum was going to the shops with a list for Mrs Lloyd, who lives next door. She'd had flu and couldn't get out. Can you see what she wants and which shops they will find the things in?

 Dear Jesus, please show me how I can help my neighbours.

In the supermarket they met Susan, one of the big girls from church. She works in the supermarket during the holidays and was busy stacking the shelves, but she stopped to help Mum find Mrs Lloyd's favourite tea.

Make a collage.
Cut out pictures of food from magazines. Stick to large sheet of paper.

 Thank You, God, for friends who help us.

 Psalm 16:5-6

After the shopping, it was into the post office to collect Mrs Lloyd's pension and to post a parcel to Grandpa. It's his birthday next weekend.

Follow the lines to see who gets the parcels.

 **Thank You, God, for all the different people who work in the post office.**

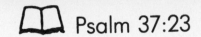

On their way out they met Jean who delivers the post. She was off on her bike with the second round.

Cut out letters to post in your post box.

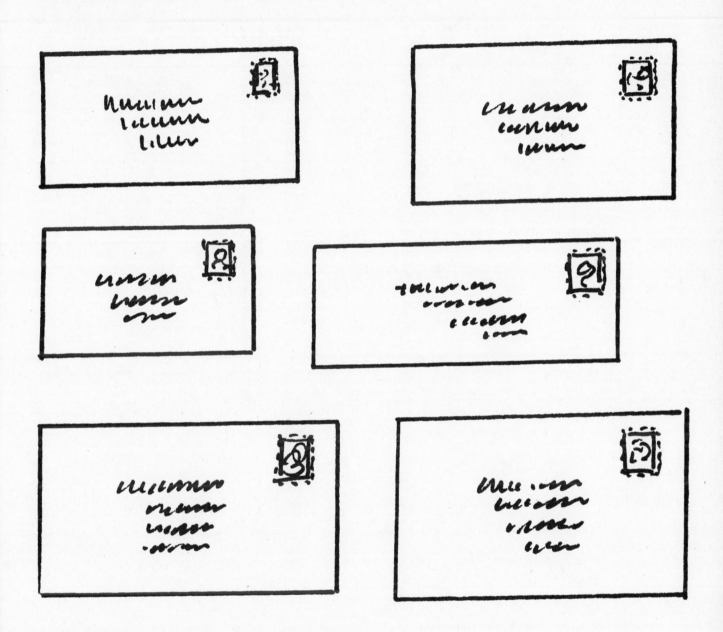

 **Dear Jesus, please take care of postmen and women as they go from house to house.**

Next stop was the launderette to collect Mrs Lloyd's washing. Her son had dropped it off on his way to work. As they arrived, the lady was just folding it and putting it back in the bag. Ben and Kate enjoyed watching the machines going round – they were so much bigger than the one they had at home.

Find six differences in these two pictures.

 Thank You, God, that we can share in helping.

There was a wedding in the town of Cana in Galilee. Jesus' mother was there. When the wine had given out, Jesus' mother said to him, "They have no wine left." Jesus' mother then told the servants, "Do whatever he tells you."

Colour-in

 Dear Jesus, please show me how to ask for Your help.

Jesus said to the servants, "Fill these jars with water." They filled them to the brim, and then he told them, "Now draw some water out and take it to the man in charge of the feast." They took him the water, which now had turned into wine, and he tasted it. He did not know where this wine had come from so he called the bridegroom and said to him, "Everyone else serves the best wine first, and after the guests have had plenty to drink, he serves the ordinary wine. But you have kept the best wine until now!"

Colour-in

 Thank You, Jesus, that Your miracles still help people today.

By the time they got home it was lunch-time, so Mum sent Ben and Kate round to Mrs Lloyd's while she prepared lunch. Mrs Lloyd was feeling much better. She gave them both a rosy apple to say 'thank you' for their help.

Find six apples in the picture.

 Dear Jesus, I'm glad I can help other people.

📖 Proverbs 8:22-23

After lunch Mum had to take Ben and Kate to the dentist for a check-up. They brushed their teeth carefully before thy went and were looking forward to riding in the chair. Ben had to have a small filling. It didn't hurt very much and the dentist said it would stop him from getting toothache, which would hurt much more.

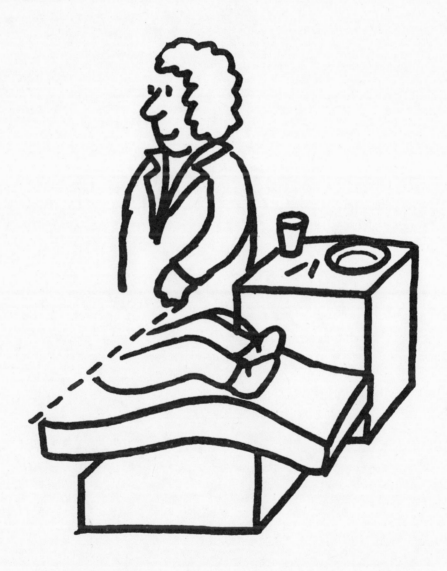

See back of book – 12 – for 'chair', cut out, cut slot to move.

 Dear Jesus, help me to take care of my teeth.

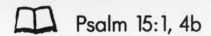

On the way home they stopped to look at the fire engines. Suddenly, bells started ringing – the station doors opened and two fire engines roared out. Ben was excited and wondered where the fire was, but Kate was worried that someone might have been hurt.

Cut out 'light'. Use strip (see back of book – 13). Colour this section blue. Slot through and slide left and right.

 Dear God, please take care of firemen as they fight fires.

Nan Drew came for tea and the children told her all about the fire engines. After tea they all watched the News on the television. The fire had been in a big empty warehouse. No one had been hurt, but it had taken the firemen quite a long time to put the fire out.

Use string or wool for hose

 Thank You, Jesus, for brave firemen.

There was another item on the News about a shipwreck. The boat was on its way back to port with a good catch of fish when it hit some rocks and began to sink.

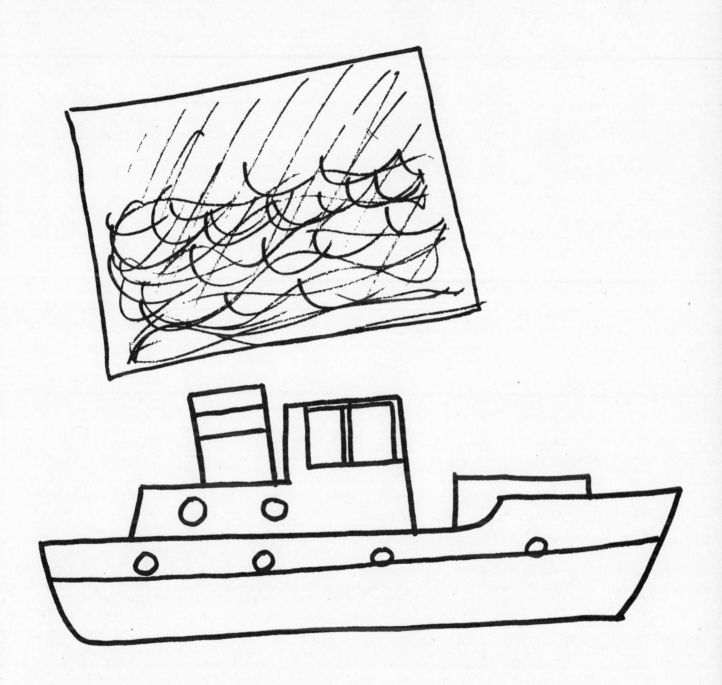

Draw or finger paint a stormy sea picture and stick on ship.

Thank You, Jesus, for people who go out in boats to catch fish for us.

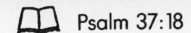 Psalm 37:18

A lifeboat was called out and the fishing-boat crew were winched aboard.

Colour-in, cut out lifeboat (see back of book – 14) and slot through.

 **Thank You, God, for people who go to sea to help others.**

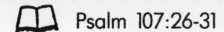

One of the fishermen had been injured when the boat hit the rocks. He was taken to hospital by helicopter.

Colour-in, make hole, thread through wool, stick person on wool (see back of book – 15).

 Thank You, God, for helicopters and the people who fly them.

Nan was babysitting for them that evening while Mum and Dad went out. She pointed out how these different people helped. At bedtime she told them a Bible story that showed how much Jesus cares and helps us too!

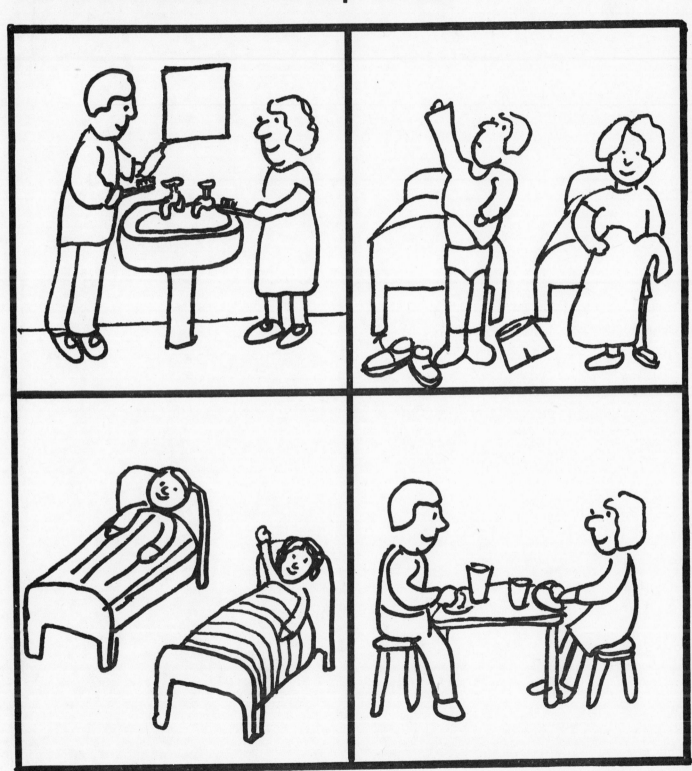

Put the pictures in the right order.

 Dear Jesus, please help me to be good when I have a babysitter.

Jesus got out of the boat, and when he saw the large crowd, his heart was filled with pity for them, and he healed those who were ill. That evening his disciples came to him and said, "It is already very late, and this is a lonely place. Send the people away and let them go to the villages to buy food for themselves." "They don't have to leave," answered Jesus. "You yourselves give them something to eat!" "All we have here are five loaves and two fish," they replied.

Colour-in

 Dear Jesus, help me to be willing to share what I have.

"Then bring them here to me," Jesus said. He ordered the people to sit down on the grass; then he took the five loaves and the two fish, looked up to heaven, and gave thanks to God. He broke the loaves and gave them to the disciples, and the disciples gave them to the people. Everyone ate and had enough. Then the disciples took up twelve baskets full of what was left over. The number of men who ate was about five thousand, not counting the women and children.

Colour-in

 Thank You, Jesus, that I have enough to eat.

Then Jesus made the disciples get into the boat and go on ahead to the other side of the lake, while he sent the people away. After sending the people away, he went up a hill by himself to pray. When evening came, Jesus was there alone; and by this time the boat was far out in the lake, tossed about by the waves, because the wind was blowing against it.

Colour-in

 Dear Jesus, please take care of people at sea.

Between three and six o'clock in the morning Jesus came to the disciples, walking on the water. When they saw him walking on the water, they were terrified. "It's a ghost!" they said, and screamed with fear. Jesus spoke to them at once. "Courage!" he said. "It is I. Don't be afraid!" Then Peter spoke up. "Lord, if it is really you, order me to come out on the water to you."

Colour-in

 Help me, God, to be brave when the weather is stormy.

"Come!" answered Jesus. So Peter got out of the boat and started walking on the water to Jesus. But when he noticed the strong wind, he was afraid and started to sink down in the water. "Save me, Lord!" he cried. At once Jesus reached out and grabbed hold of him and said, "How little faith you have! Why did you doubt?" They both got into the boat, and the wind died down. Then the disciples in the boat worshipped Jesus. "Truly you are the Son of God!" they exclaimed.

Colour-in

 Thank You, Jesus, that You are always there to help me.

At the Zoo

**Fun to Use Bible Activity Book
to help you grow with God**

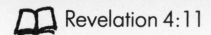

Everyone was in a rush. Dad was late for work and he had to take Matthew to Nan's on the way. Mum was making the breakfast, packing a picnic and trying to do Kate's hair. They were dropping Kate at playgroup on the way to Ben's school. His class was going to the zoo and Mum was coming too!

Draw your favourite picnic foods.

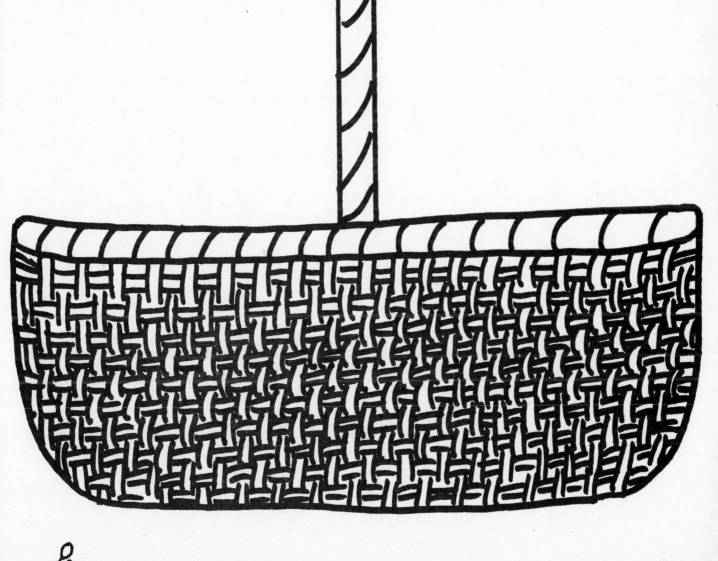

Dear Jesus, please let me be helpful when everyone is in a rush.

Job 38:14

At last it was time to leave. Mrs Court, Ben's teacher, had checked the register and everyone climbed onto the bus. Ben stared out of the window as they passed houses, shops and factories, then fields, trees and farms. Suddenly the bus stopped and they were there! Out piled everyone, two by two, "Just like the animals going into the ark," thought Ben.

Cut slots and pull strip through.
See last page for strip.

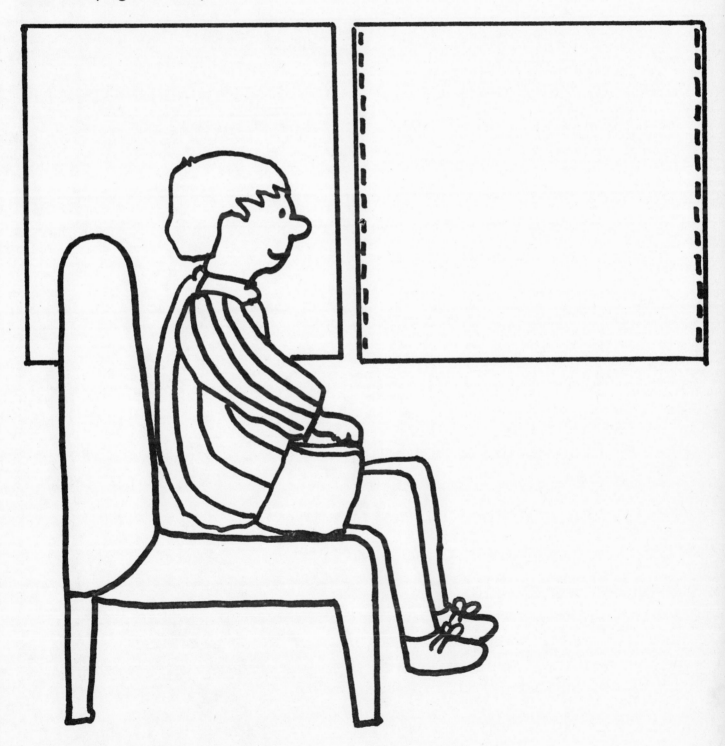

Thank You, God, for the countryside.

 Gen 7:1, 8a, 9

"The Lord said to Noah, 'Go into the boat with your whole family; I have found that you are the only one in all the world who does what is right.' A male and a female of every kind of animal and bird went into the boat with Noah, as God had commanded."

Colour in.

 Dear Jesus, please help me to be obedient.

"Seven days later the flood came. The flood continued for forty days, and the water became deep enough for the boat to float. The water became deeper, and the boat drifted on the surface. Everything on earth that breathed died."

Colour in.

 Dear Jesus, please take care of people when there are floods.

"God had not forgotten Noah and all the animals with him in the boat; he caused a wind to blow, and the water started going down. On the seventeenth day of the seventh month the boat came to rest on a mountain in the Ararat range. After forty days Noah opened a window and sent out a raven. It did not come back, but kept flying around until the water was completely gone."

Colour in.

 Dear Jesus, please take care of people who travel by boat.

Gen 8:8–11

"Meanwhile, Noah sent out a dove to see if the water had gone down, but since the water still covered all the land, the dove did not find a place to alight. It flew back to the boat, and Noah reached out and took it in. He waited another seven days and sent out the dove again. It returned to him in the evening with a fresh olive leaf in its beak. So Noah knew that the water had gone down."

Colour in.

Thank You, God, for beautiful birds.

"So Noah went out of the boat with his wife, his sons, and their wives. All the animals and birds went out of the boat in groups of their own kind."

Colour in.

 Thank You, God, that You always take care of me.

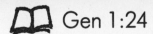 Gen 1:24

Once through the gates the class split into groups. There was so much to look at, all those animals — monkeys swinging from branch to branch, giraffes with long necks, lions with fluffy manes and, of course, the elephants with their long trunks.

Colour in shapes with dots to find the animal.

 Thank You, God, for making all the animals.

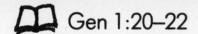 Gen 1:20–22

Next came the birds, brightly coloured parrots, tiny finches, toucans with their strange beaks and peacocks with their beautiful tails.

Finger paint or draw the peacock tail.

 Thank You, God, for all You have made.

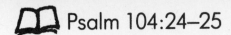 Psalm 104:24–25

At 11 o'clock all the groups met up to go into the aquarium. Inside, they saw so many fish, all different shapes and sizes and, as well, there were starfish, crabs, sea horses, and even a huge octopus with lots of legs.

Stick on silver paper and scraps. Cover with cellophane.

Thank You, God, for fish and everything that lives in the water.

Proverbs 30:24–28

After the fish was the insect house. Some of the girls were scared and Mum Ross wasn't very keen. Even though she knew God had made them, Mum didn't like things with lots of legs that scuttled about, especially spiders, so she offered to walk the girls around the pond instead.

Make a pipe cleaner spider.
Bind with wool or string to make body.

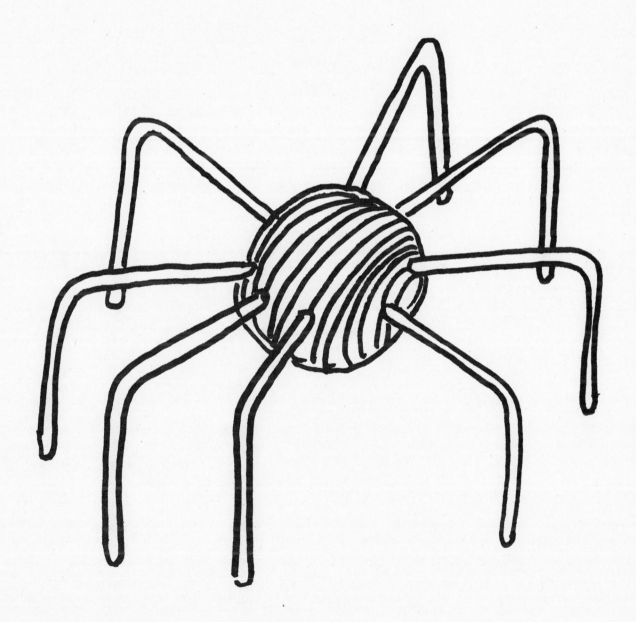

Dear Jesus, please take care of me when I'm scared.

Ben enjoyed the insects though, especially the huge butterflies and the bees inside their hive making a comb.

Make a butterfly by folding a piece of paper in half. Paint on one half and when still wet re-fold and press to make whole butterfly.

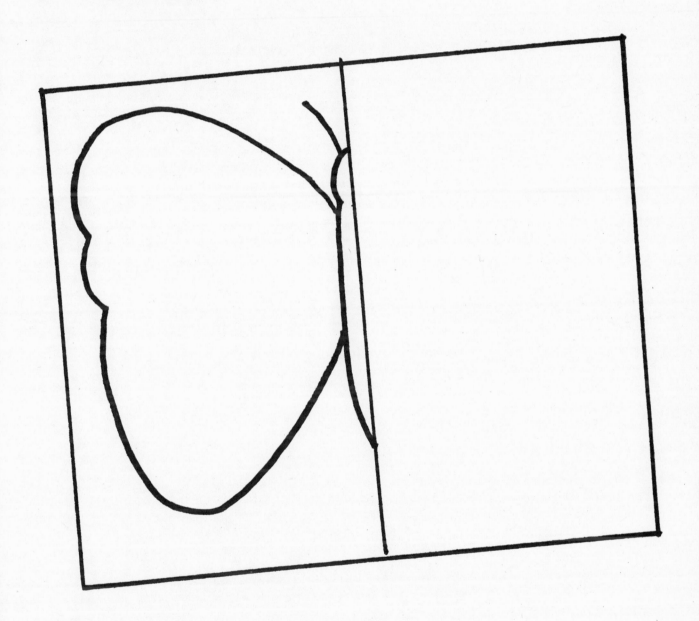

 Thank You, God, for all Your creatures.

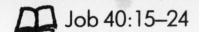

Just before lunch came the reptile house. Now it was Ben's turn to be worried. He wasn't sure about the slithering, slimy ones. But it was all right, everything was behind glass. There were even baby crocodiles, as well as snakes, frogs, turtles and lizards.

Make a frog.
Cut paper strip for body and narrow
strips for arms. Fold and glue on arms.

Stick on eyes. Use card for feet.
See last page for eyes and template for feet.

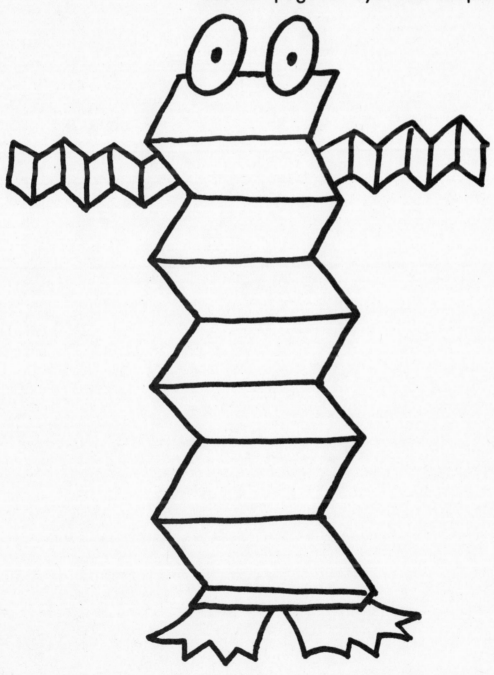

 Dear Jesus, please help me to be brave.

At last it was lunchtime. Mum's group, including Ben, decided to eat in the Pets' corner. As they ate, they watched the keeper taking care of the animals. He cleaned out the rabbits' and guinea pigs' enclosure just like Ben's class had to clean the cages at school. Then he gave them fresh cabbage and carrots too.

Cut out to make a jigsaw.

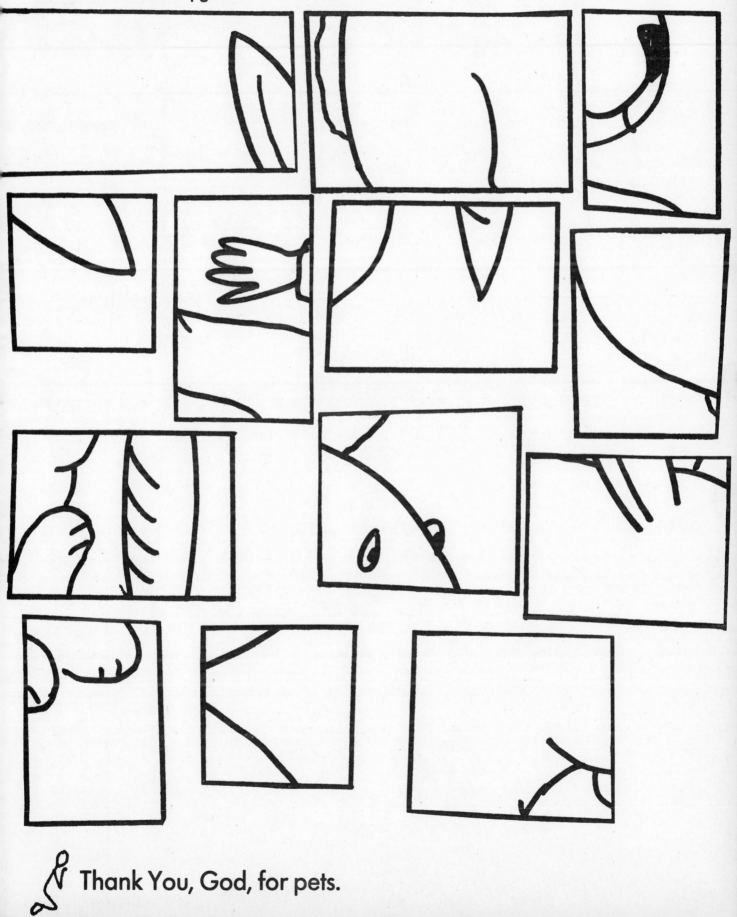

Thank You, God, for pets.

 Psalm 104:10–12

Another keeper was cleaning the aviary. There were feathers everywhere, then she replaced the water and filled up the seed exactly the way Ben did for his bird Sparks at home.

Find six differences in these pictures.

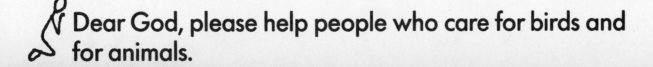 Dear God, please help people who care for birds and for animals.

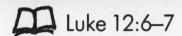 Luke 12:6–7

When they had all finished eating Ben tipped his crumbs down for the sparrows. Mum collected all her group together and led them to the place where they would meet the others.

Draw a line to the same birds.

 Dear Jesus, please help me to take care of my pets.

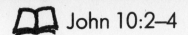 John 10:2–4

"The man who goes in through the gate is the shepherd of the sheep. The gatekeeper opens the gate for him; the sheep hear his voice as he calls his own sheep by name, and he leads them out. When he has brought them out, he goes ahead of them, and the sheep follow him, because they know his voice."

Colour in.

 Dear Jesus, please help me to follow You.

📖 John 10:11–15

"I am the good shepherd, who is willing to die for the sheep. When the hired man, who is not a shepherd and does not own the sheep, sees a wolf coming, he leaves the sheep and runs away; so the wolf snatches the sheep and scatters them. The hired man runs away because he is only a hired man and does not care about the sheep. I am the good shepherd. As the Father knows me and I know the Father, in the same way I know my sheep and they know me. And I am willing to die for them."

Colour in.

 Dear Lord, I'm glad You know me.

Just as Mum's group met up with the class, Mrs Squires, Ben's dinner lady, rushed up. One of her group was missing. Alan Greig had just disappeared.

Help Mrs. Squire to find Andrew.

🙏 **Dear Jesus, please take care of people who are lost and alone.**

 Psalm 94:19.

Mrs Court told all the class to sit down on the grass while she sent two of the mums off with Mrs Squires to search. Mrs Court looked very worried, but a bit cross too.

Draw a line to put the right animal in right house.

 Dear Jesus, help me to do as I am told.

Luke 15:4–6

"Suppose one of you has a hundred sheep and loses one of them — what does he do? He leaves the other ninety-nine sheep in the pasture and goes looking for the one that got lost until he finds it. When he finds it, he is so happy that he puts it on his shoulders and carries it back home. Then he calls his friends and neighbours together and says to them, 'I am so happy I found my lost sheep. Let us celebrate!'"

Colour in.

Dear Jesus, thank You for always watching over me.

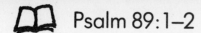

Soon they were back and Alan was with them. He had been crying. He'd wandered off to look at the bears and then couldn't find the others. Mrs Court took Alan to one side, spoke to him firmly, then smiled, gave him a hug and turned back to the class – "Come on everyone, we're off to meet the keeper."

Make a bear out of a brown paper bag.
Stuff the bag with paper, seal end with sticky tape.
Draw on a face. Cut out and stick on
ears. Use paper for legs.

 Dear Jesus, thank You that You always forgive me.

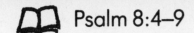 Psalm 8:4–9

The children all followed Mrs Court into a big hut. It was quite dark inside. There were pictures and maps on the walls, and some boxes covered with cloths. Everyone was very quiet.

Draw from dot to dot to find animal.

Thank You, God, for quiet times.

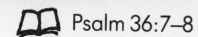 Psalm 36:7–8

Mr Bryant, the keeper, welcomed everyone to the zoo. Then he asked the children why they thought the animals were there. Ben put up his hand quickly, so did lots of the others. Everyone had the same answer – for people to come and look at them. Yes ....

Draw your favourite bird.

 Thank You, God, for all the people who take care of animals.

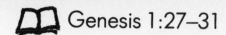 Genesis 1:27–31

Mr Bryant went on to tell the children there were other reasons for zoos too. In some countries there are not many wild animals left, so they need protecting and taking care of. Ben remembered Uncle Jack telling him that in Africa lots of elephants are killed so that their ivory tusks can be sold to carve.

Make a 3D animal.

Fold a sheet of card in half. Draw on animal, colour in and cut out.

 Dear Jesus, forgive us for being greedy.

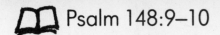

Mr Bryant then lifted off one of the cloths. Underneath was a red and blue parrot in a cage. In South America, he told the children, the forests are being cut down for roads and farming so there is nowhere for the parrots to live.

Stick on scraps or coloured paper.

Dear Jesus, please let all the world care about our animals and birds.

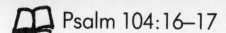 Psalm 104:16–17

On the wall was a picture of some pandas eating bamboo. Mr Bryant showed the class on a map of China that there is not so much bamboo grown now.

Stick on drinking straws or tissue for bamboo.

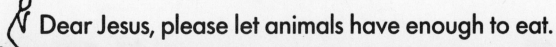 Dear Jesus, please let animals have enough to eat.

Last of all, Mr Bryant lifted another cloth, put his hand in a tank and lifted out a snake. Ben moved closer to Mum. The keeper explained that snakes weren't really slimy and they are often killed so their skins can be used for shoes and handbags. Then Mr Bryant said goodbye and invited the children to stroke the snake, now hanging around his neck, as they went out. Ben did, he was surprised — it wasn't slimy at all!

Make a bouncy snake.

Draw a snake shape onto a piece of paper, colour in, cut out.

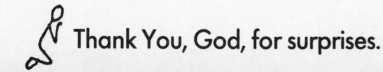 Thank You, God, for surprises.

On the way back to the bus there was just enough time to watch the penguins and seals being fed. They were so funny — the way they walked and then dived under the water after the fish.

Make a toilet roll penguin. See last page for beak, etc.

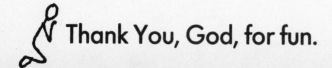 Thank You, God, for fun.

📖 Psalm 50:10–11

Back in the coach, Ben felt very tired. He had so much to remember to tell Dad and Nan, Kate and Matthew. All those different animals that God had made. Soon Ben was asleep against Mum's arm, dreaming of elephants, frogs, parrots, rabbits, monkeys and lots more too.

Find four animals and two birds in this picture.

 Thank You, God, for Your wonderful world.

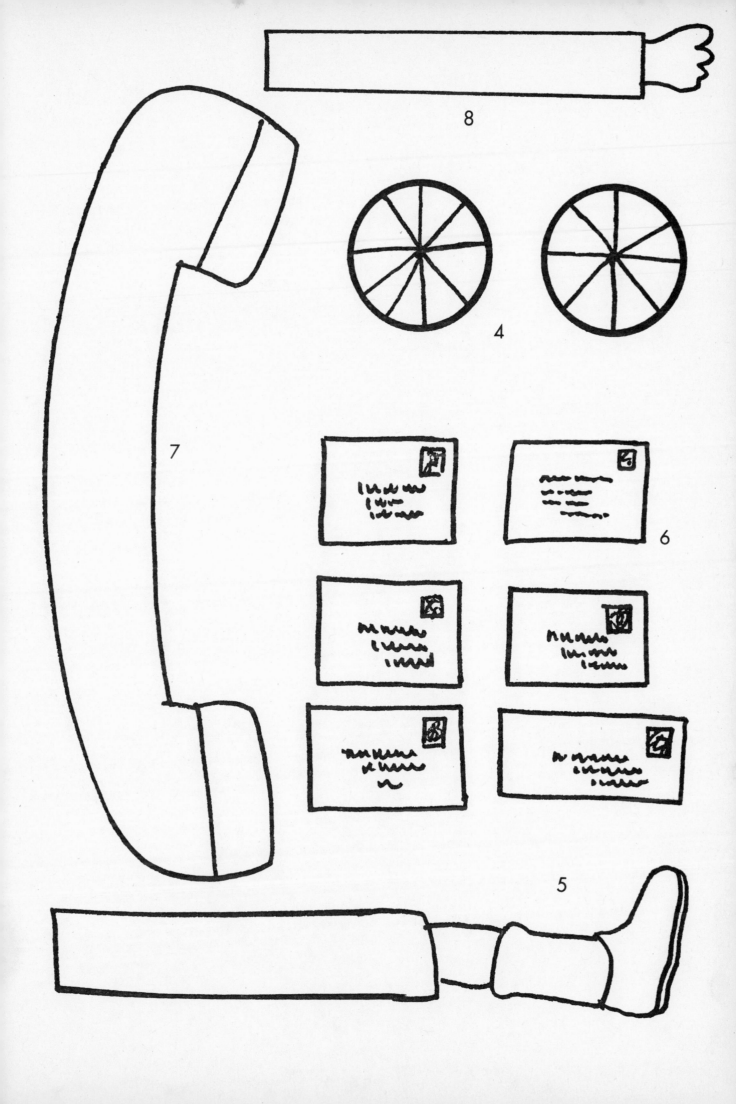

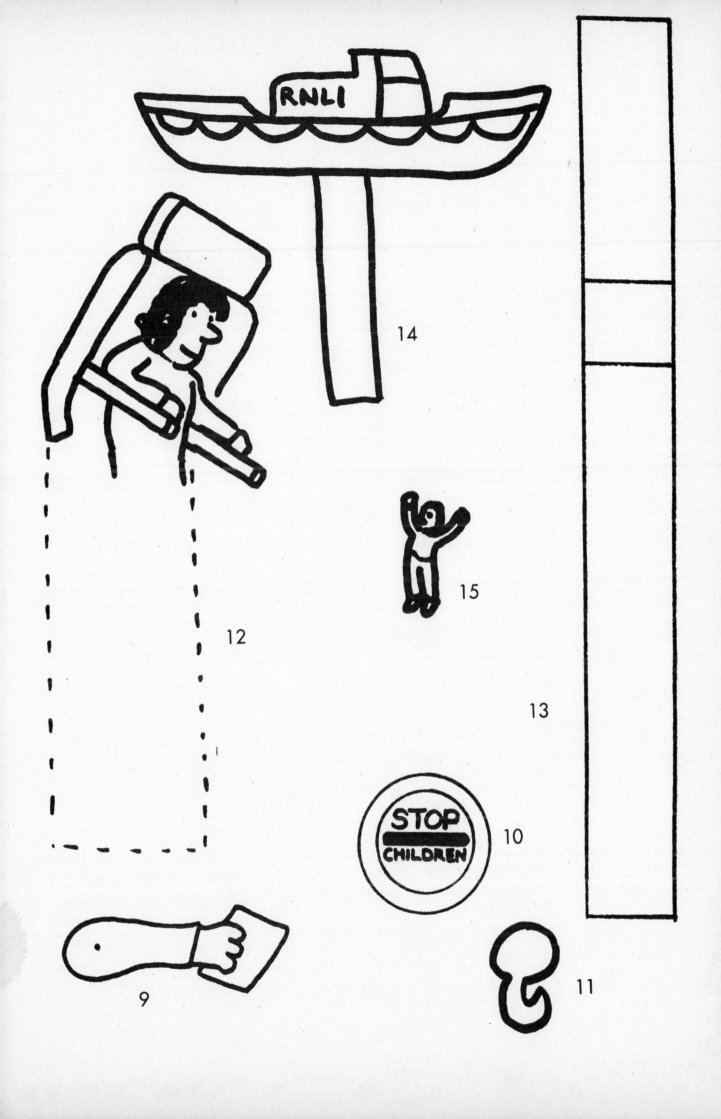

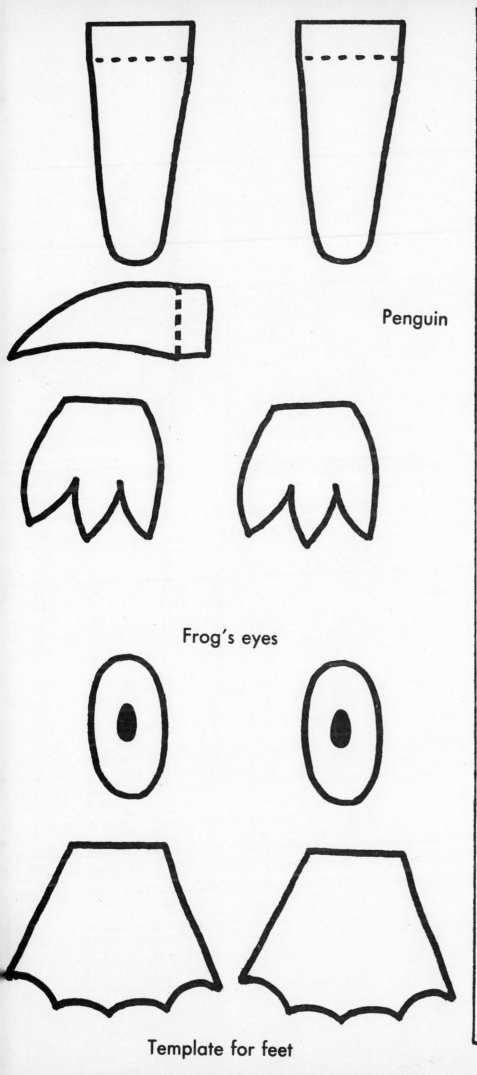

Penguin

Frog's eyes

Template for feet

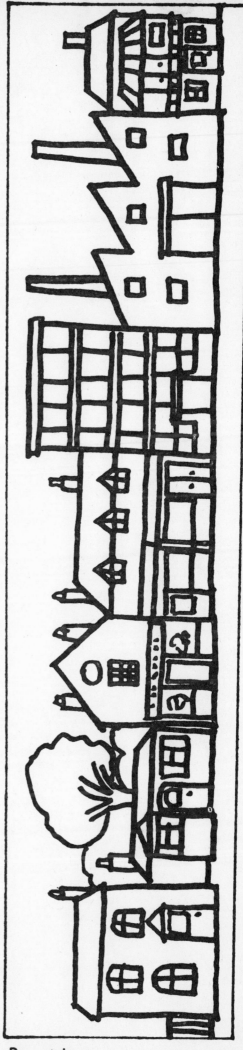

Bus strip